FIGHTING TO SURVIVE THE POLAR REGIONS
TERRIFYING TRUE STORIES

by Michael Burgan

COMPASS POINT BOOKS
a capstone imprint

Fighting to Survive is published by
Compass Point Books, an imprint of Capstone.
1710 Roe Crest Drive, North Mankato, Minnesota 56003
www.capstonepub.com

**Library of Congress Cataloging-in-Publication Data is available
on the Library of Congress website**
ISBN: 978-0-7565-6433-9 (hardcover)
ISBN: 978-0-7565-6570-1 (paperback)
ISBN: 978-0-7565-6434-6 (ebook pdf)

Summary: Describes the terrifying true stories of explorers and others who survived the
extreme climate, starvation, rough terrain, and other dangers in Earth's polar regions.

Editorial Credits
Aaron J. Sautter, editor; Terri Poburka, designer; Morgan Walters, media researcher;
Kathy McColley, production specialist

Photo Credits
Alamy: Alpha Stock, 34, Charles Polidano/Touch The Skies, 24, Historic Collection, 43,
IanDagnall Computing, 51, 59, Image Vault, 31, Pictorial Press Ltd, 55, Radharc Images,
56–57; Bridgeman Images: Byron Company, 33; Getty Images: Mansell, 9, Print Collector,
46–47, 48, Royal Geographical Society, 44; iStockphoto: DieterMeyrl, Cover (man);
Newscom: Adam Woolfitt/robertharding, 23, Album/Kurwenal/Prisma, 53, Design
Pics/Ken Welsh, 13, Peter Barritt/Photoshot, 7, State Library of New South Wales/Cover
Images, 4; Shutterstock: ANL, 15, Denis Radermecker, 17, Douglas Olivares, 21, Isaac
Marzioli, design element throughout, Miloje, design element throughout, outdoorsman,
29, Peter Hermes Furian, 10, 19, 26, robert mcgillivray, Cover (landscape), xpixel, design
element throughout; Wikimedia: Bartlett, Robert A. (1916) Last Voyage of the Karluk, 40,
Finetooth, 39; Wikipedia: Bartlett & Hale, The Last Voyage of the Karluk, 37

Printed and bound in the USA.
PA99

TABLE OF CONTENTS

INTRODUCTION

At the top of the world, an invisible circle stretches several hundred miles around the North Pole. Humans have lived in this region, called the Arctic Circle, for tens of thousands of years. They learned to survive in its cold and snowy climate by hunting and fishing. But for some who have dared to explore the region, ice and cold have proved deadly. On some Arctic expeditions, only a few people survived journeys that doomed their companions.

On the opposite end of the globe, an even colder land surrounds the South Pole. Antarctica is one of Earth's seven continents, and its climate is the harshest on the planet. Blizzard winds there can reach 200 miles (322 kilometers) per hour. Temperatures often plummet to minus 100 degrees Fahrenheit (minus 73 degrees Celsius) or more. Ice sheets in Antarctica can be more than 1 mile (1.6 km) thick. Unlike the Arctic, no one settled in Antarctica until 1898, when the first scientists set up a base to study the weather and wildlife there. But even before then, brave explorers made the difficult journey to Antarctica. Some wanted to reach the South Pole. Others sought to map the geography. Even today, some people attempt to ski across the remote southern continent. They love the adventure of pushing themselves to withstand the extreme cold and isolation.

Whether they're explorers, scientists, or sailors, several people have survived the harsh conditions of the polar regions. In the stories ahead, you'll meet people who could have died from starvation or the bitter cold during missions that went wrong. But in most cases, their incredible courage and skill, along with some luck, helped them survive the most extreme locations on Earth.

In the early 1900s, few people had the strength and courage to explore Earth's harsh polar regions.

AND THEN THERE WAS ONE
DOUGLAS MAWSON

With 16 dogs, two sledges, and almost a ton of food and supplies, Australian scientist Douglas Mawson was ready. On November 10, 1912, he set off to explore the northern coast of Antarctica. No human had ever gone there before, and Mawson wanted to map the area and collect mineral samples.

Joining him on the expedition were Xavier Mertz and Belgrave Ninnis. The three had sailed to Antarctica on the ship *Aurora* as members of a much larger team called the Australasian Antarctic Expedition. Its mission was to explore and chart 2,000 miles (3,200 km) of Antarctica's coastline that lay south of Australia. Mawson, the mission leader, was no stranger to the world's southern continent. He had explored part of it in 1908 on an expedition led by Ernest Shackleton, who had hoped to become the first person to reach the South Pole. After that first trip, Mawson decided he wanted to return to Antarctica to focus more on science.

As Mawson and his partners set off with their dogs, they hoped to reach a point about 350 miles (563 km) southeast of the expedition's main base at Cape Denison. They had to get there and back by January 15, 1913. That day, the *Aurora* would return to pick up the expedition members and bring them back to Australia. The men had just enough food to last for the two months they would be on the ice. And if they missed the ship, they would have to wait another eight months for it to return in the spring. South of the equator, the seasons are reversed, so spring begins in September.

A few days out from the main base, even as summer approached, Mawson's team got a taste of Antarctica's extreme weather. A blizzard with winds of 80 miles (129 km) per hour kept them in their tent for two days. When they could move, they had to travel over rough sastrugi.

These windblown snow ridges look like sand dunes. Even worse were the crevasses. These gaps in glacial ice are sometimes hidden by a thin layer of snow. When people try to cross over these "snow bridges," they can easily fall through into the gaping holes below. Mawson saw the danger of a crevasse on November 20, when some of the team's dogs plunged into one. Luckily, the men were able to pull them back to safety.

Roald Amundsen and his team of sled dogs at the South Pole on December 14, 1911

DID YOU KNOW?

Douglas Mawson was just one of several explorers traveling across Antarctica in 1911 and 1912. When Mawson left Australia in December 1911, Roald Amundsen and Robert Falcon Scott were each attempting to reach the South Pole. Mawson had met Scott previously in 1910. The explorer had asked Mawson to join his expedition. Mawson said no, since Scott wasn't interested in exploring Antarctica's northern coast. Mawson later learned that Scott had lost to Amundsen in the race to the South Pole. Scott and the rest of his five-man team died on their return journey.

A DANGEROUS CREVASSE

The danger of falling into crevasses and losing dogs only seemed to grow as the team went on. Ninnis started to fall into a crevasse but was able to pull himself out. One sledge nearly fell into another crevasse, but its runners caught in the ice before it went too far. However, the team lost several dogs. One wandered off and was never seen again. The team also killed some dogs that couldn't keep up the pace. Their meat became food for the remaining dogs.

Despite the setbacks, after about a month, the team had covered almost 300 miles (483 km). On December 14, the men woke to sun and relatively warm temperatures, about 21° F (-6° C). That day Mertz was traveling on skis when he signaled that he was crossing a crevasse. Mawson passed a warning back to Ninnis, who was guiding the last sledge. Mawson then continued on. But then he saw that Mertz had stopped and was looking behind him. When Mawson turned to look, Ninnis and his dogs had vanished.

Mawson and Mertz went back to the crevasse. A snow bridge had given way, revealing a gap about 11 feet (3.4 meters) wide. When Mawson looked down, he could see one of the dogs on a shelf of ice, some 150 feet (46 m) below. But there was no sign of Ninnis. Mawson and Mertz shouted down into the gap, but they didn't get a response. Ninnis was dead.

The team didn't just lose a trusted companion. The sledge Ninnis was steering had carried most of the team's food and important equipment. Mawson figured they had enough food left to last about 10 days. That night the men boiled their empty food bags to get the last crumbs out of them. They fed leather to the remaining dogs.

The next day Mertz and Mawson turned around and retraced their path back to the third sledge they had left behind days before. They used part of the sledge and a tent cover to make a crude shelter. They realized they would have to slowly kill the dogs for food, or they wouldn't survive the long journey back to the base. They faced, as Mawson later wrote, "a fight with Death," and only luck would decide if they won.

The group suffered a terrible blow when Ninnis's sledge fell into a deep crevasse. Along with Ninnis, the team lost several dogs, the tent, clothing, and most of the food.

GROWING WEAKER

Day after day, the two men traveled west. Some days were clear. But other days the snow whipped around them. They ate only the smallest amounts of food, hoping to make what they had last as long as possible. As they grew weaker and the number of dogs fell to three, they threw away what they could to lighten the load on the sledge. More than a week after Ninnis's death, they still hadn't reached the halfway point back to the base.

On December 28, Mawson and Mertz killed the last dog. But its meat lasted only for a few days. As the New Year began, Mertz showed signs of failing health. His energy faded, his fingers were frostbitten, and patches of skin fell off his legs. He stopped eating solid food, getting down only some powdered milk mixed with water.

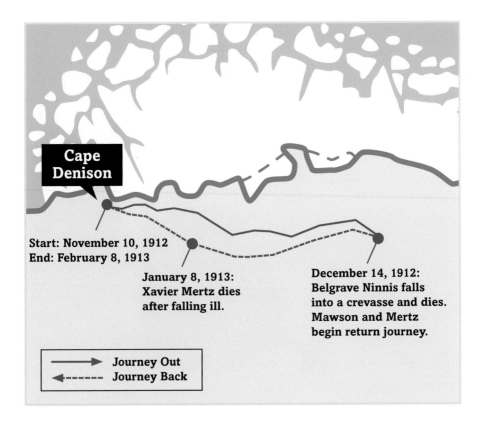

Cape Denison

Start: November 10, 1912
End: February 8, 1913

January 8, 1913:
Xavier Mertz dies
after falling ill.

December 14, 1912:
Belgrave Ninnis falls
into a crevasse and dies.
Mawson and Mertz
begin return journey.

→ Journey Out
◄----- Journey Back

By January 7, Mertz's poor health slowed the men down to only about 1 mile (1.6 km) each day. At this rate, they would never reach the base by January 15. Still, Mawson knew he couldn't leave Mertz behind. That day, however, Mertz had what Mawson called fits. He was too weak to even leave his sleeping bag to relieve himself. Early on the morning of January 8, Mertz died. Mawson would have to cross the remaining frozen miles alone.

BATTLING PAIN AND THE WEATHER

To try to make the rest of the journey faster, Mawson used his pocketknife to cut the remaining sledge in half. He then made a sail, partly out of Mertz's clothing. He hoped the strong Antarctic winds would push the sledge along the ice. But bad weather kept Mawson stuck.

Finally on January 11, he headed out again. But traveling was very painful. The bottom layer of skin had peeled away from his feet, exposing raw skin underneath. He bandaged his feet as best he could and tried to ignore the pain. He managed to cover several miles each day when the wind and snow weren't too bad. But he knew he wouldn't reach the base in time. When he made it there—*if* he made it there at all—the *Aurora* would have sailed.

Still, despite his pain and growing hunger, Mawson trudged on. He knew the danger of falling into a crevasse, but there was no way to avoid one hidden by snow. One day he did plunge into a crevasse. Only his sledge, which became stuck in the snow, stopped him from falling even deeper. He held onto a rope attached to the sledge and began to climb up. When he had almost reached the top, the snow around the edge crumbled, and he went down again.

A LIFESAVING DISCOVERY

Mawson dangled on the rope in the icy hole. He felt too weak to climb again. But he wasn't ready to die. He found the strength for one more climb. This time, he made it to the top. Then he collapsed and passed out. When he woke again, a light dusting of snow covered his body.

Mawson made a simple rope ladder, hoping he could use it if he fell into another crevasse. The ladder soon came in handy, as he did plunge into several more holes. Over the next week he kept moving on, with the wind sometimes pushing his sledge.

By the end of January, Mawson was covering more ground each day, but his health was worsening. His skin was coming off and his hair was falling out. The food was almost gone. Then he finally had some good luck. He spotted a black cloth covering a stack of ice blocks. Pulling back the cloth, he found a store of food left by other members of the expedition. They had searched for him and left the food behind. Reading a note that the search team had left, Mawson learned that he'd missed them by only a few hours. But at least now he knew he was getting closer, and he wouldn't starve.

For several days, Mawson took shelter in a snow cave the expedition members had dug. They called it Aladdin's Cave, and it was only about 5 miles (8 km) from the base. Mawson knew he was close to home. The cave contained food and supplies. But Mawson was still missing one tool that would help him cover the last icy miles—crampons. People slip these spiked metal devices over their boots to walk on glaciers.

Going through the items in the cave, Mawson made his own crude crampons with screws. On February 8, he set off down a hill of ice. Within several hours, men working outside at the base spotted him and ran to greet him. They told him that the *Aurora* had just left to pick up some expedition members at a camp 1,500 miles (2,414 km) to the west. No one knew if the ship would return before winter began.

As it turned out, the *Aurora* didn't return until the following December. But at the base camp, Mawson and the others had shelter and enough food to survive the Antarctic winter. Mawson had suffered terrible physical and mental pain from his ordeal on Antarctica's harsh landscape. But after several weeks he recovered. Today, some people consider Mawson's survival story the greatest in the history of exploration.

When Mawson finally returned to the base camp alone, he learned that the Aurora *had already left.*

WARTIME SURVIVAL
JAN BAALSRUD EVADES THE NAZIS

On March 30, 1943, bullets ripped through the tiny rowboat carrying Jan Baalsrud and four other soldiers off the coast of Norway. The men and the rest of their team had blown up their ship, the *Brattholm*, rather than let the Germans capture it. Now, as the Nazi soldiers fired at him, Baalsrud dove into the icy waters nearly 300 miles (483 km) north of the Arctic Circle.

Norway had been under German control since 1940. It was just one of several European nations Germany conquered during World War II (1939–1945). In 1943 Baalsrud and the other Norwegian commandos had left an island near Scotland on a secret mission. They were returning to Norway aboard the *Brattholm* to blow up the Nazi troops' ferries and communications systems. But their mission was discovered, and a German warship attacked the *Brattholm* as it sat anchored near Toftefjord, Norway.

As Baalsrud jumped off the sinking rowboat, he lost his right boot and sock. He and the others swam ashore. But there was no safety there, as German soldiers followed them in a small boat. Baalsrud left the others and climbed up some rocks. He saw the Germans shoot one of his companions. His water-soaked clothing was turning into a suit of ice, but Baalsrud kept moving. Four of the Germans closed in on him. As they approached, he fired his gun. Two of the enemy soldiers fell to the snow. The other two quickly retreated.

As he pushed on, Baalsrud heard the shouts of his fellow commandos as the Germans captured them. He knew if he were caught, he could be tortured and killed. He scrambled up a snow-covered hill, hoping to find safety. His only hope for survival was to reach Sweden, located to the south. Sweden had stayed out of the war. If he reached that neutral country, Baalsrud could return to the United Kingdom and continue to fight the Germans who occupied Norway.

Jan Baalsrud in 1954

DID YOU KNOW?

Germany's occupation of the Arctic in World War II went as far as the North Pole. On an island near the pole, they built a secret weather station. German troops and meteorologists were based there for about a year.

HELP FROM LOCAL RESIDENTS

But reaching Sweden meant covering many snow-covered, mountainous miles without food or proper clothing. In this remote part of Norway, Baalsrud would need the help of Norwegians who wanted their country to be free. He knew he could also meet Norwegians who worked for the Germans and would turn him in. For now, though, his main concern was to avoid the German troops searching for him.

Baalsrud's first move was returning to the freezing water and swimming to a small island. He hid in a hole so the German soldiers wouldn't see him. As the day went on, he swam to several large rocks where he hoped the enemy wouldn't spot him. His last swim took him to another island. His exposed right foot was bleeding from a bullet wound he hadn't noticed before. The foot was also frostbitten, and he felt the chilling effects of the cold water through his entire body.

Then Baalsrud had his first stroke of luck. He spotted some children playing on the shore in Toftefjord near the island. He called out to them, and they rowed to the island. One girl, Dina Pedersen, decided to take him to her home.

The Pedersens soon learned that Baalsrud had been part of the failed mission against the Germans. Over the next several days, they and other families gave him warm clothes and food as he moved from house to house. The local people he met didn't question him, and he said little about why he was on the run. Baalsrud didn't want his helpers to face any trouble from the Gestapo, the German secret police. In between visits with helpful locals, Baalsrud trudged on alone, sometimes through heavy snowstorms.

On April 3 Baalsrud reached the home of Einar Sorensen. The Sorensen family fed him and gave him ski boots and skis to make his journey a little easier. Sorensen also offered to take Baalsrud to the mainland so he could continue his journey to Sweden. On April 5 he

Avalanches happen when a snowpack on a mountain becomes unstable and breaks loose. These dangerous masses of snow, ice, and rock race down mountains at high speed, often destroying everything in their path.

began to ski cross-country, traveling that night on roads covered with snow. As morning neared, he came upon a group of German soldiers. Baalsrud stayed calm and simply skied past them.

To avoid meeting more Germans, Baalsrud changed his course and headed for some nearby mountains. Suddenly, the wind picked up and snow began to fall. Before long, Baalsrud was in the middle of a fierce snowstorm. Although the cold gripped his entire body and his right foot ached, he kept going.

With fog and snow all around, Baalsrud couldn't see the nearby mountains—or the avalanche that raced toward him. But he could hear it. The roar of moving ice and snow was deafening as it closed around him. Before he could move, the avalanche knocked him off his feet and carried him to the valley below.

A PAINFUL TREK

The avalanche buried him in deep snow and left him with a concussion. The rushing snow had stripped off one of his skis and broken the other. Even worse, his hat, gloves, and food were also buried somewhere in the mounds of snow around him.

Despite his head injury and losing his skis, Baalsrud picked himself up and began trudging through the snow. He walked through the night, not sure where he was going or which direction he should take. His hands turned blue from the cold, and his boots couldn't keep his feet warm in the deep snow. But he knew he had to keep walking, or he would die. At times he became delirious and thought he heard the voices of his fellow commandos back at Toftefjord.

In spite of the extreme cold, Baalsrud pushed on until he reached the village of Furuflaten. There, he found a small house. He scratched along its wall and tried to open the door. Inside, another family named Pedersen heard the noises and opened the door. They saw an ice-covered Baalsrud, his face scratched and bloodied from the avalanche. His eyes were swollen, and he could barely see. But Baalsrud could open them just enough to see some leftover food on the Pedersens' table. Without saying a word, he went to the table and began shoveling food into his mouth.

Mrs. Pedersen sent for her brother, Marius Grønvoll, who lived next door. Grønvoll led the local resistance group who worked secretly against the Germans. He and the Pedersens got Baalsrud out of his icy clothes and began to warm him.

Toftefjorden, Norway

Manndalen, Norway

Furuflaten, Norway

Barents Sea

Norwegian Sea

ARCTIC CIRCLE

White Sea

Boden, Sweden

SWEDEN

FINLAND

Lake Onega

Gulf of Bothnia

Lake Ladoga

HELSINKI

Gulf of Finland

NORWAY

OSLO

Aland Islands (FIN.)

TALLINN

RUSSIA

STOCKHOLM

ESTONIA

Volga

North Sea

Skagerrak

Kattegat

Gotland (SWE.)

LATVIA

Baalsrud evaded enemy soldiers, lived through an avalanche, and survived the Arctic's extreme cold to reach safety in Boden, Sweden more than 460 miles (740 km) away.

FACING DEATH

Grønvoll then used a sled to move Baalsrud to a barn where he could hide as he recovered. For days Baalsrud couldn't walk, and he struggled to see. He escaped a close call when two German soldiers came to the Grønvoll farm looking for hidden radios. The Germans had taken everyone's radios to prevent them from listening to news reports from England. One of the soldiers entered the barn and took a quick look in the loft where Baalsrud was hiding. But all he saw was hay.

After Baalsrud spent four days on his farm, Marius Grønvoll decided it was time to help the commando continue his journey to Sweden. He and some other resistance members put Baalsrud on a sled and pulled him to a boat on the river. The boat took him across the fjord and left him at an isolated hut. There, he could continue to recover with little danger of the enemy troops finding him. In a few days, Grønvoll and the men returned to bring more food.

More days passed. As Grønvoll tried to find a way to get Baalsrud to Sweden, a storm delayed him. Meanwhile, in his wooden hut, the wounded man watched as his toes turned black. He knew what that meant—gangrene was setting in. The frostbite from trekking through the cold had shut off the flow of blood and destroyed the skin and tissue. Baalsrud knew that the gangrene could spread throughout his body and kill him if he didn't take drastic action.

Using only some alcohol to try to kill the pain, Baalsrud took a knife and began to saw off two of his toes. He sweated and shivered as he carried out this crude operation and then fell backward onto his bed. With his hands trembling, he began to cry. Then, noticing more black spots on his foot, he cut them off too.

The next day, the weather cleared enough for Grønvoll and the others to reach the hut. They opened the door and a disgusting smell greeted them—the smell of Baalsrud's rotting flesh. The men found him on a cot and saw the bloodied stumps on his feet. "We're here to take care of you, Jan," Grønvoll said. They gave him food and cleaned his wounds.

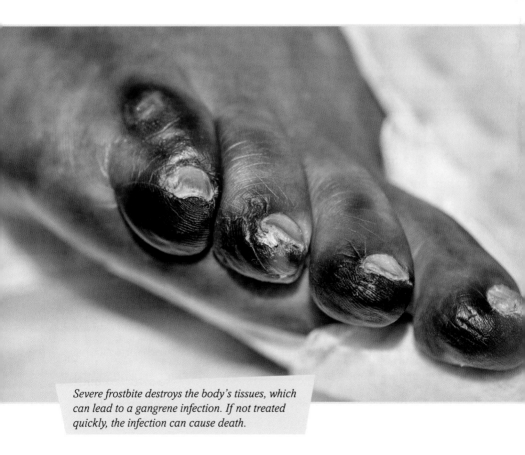

Severe frostbite destroys the body's tissues, which can lead to a gangrene infection. If not treated quickly, the infection can cause death.

THE TRIP TO SWEDEN

After treating Baalsrud's injuries, Grønvoll continued trying
to find a way to get him to Sweden. Many people helped him.
A local carpenter made a sled to transport Baalsrud across the snow.
Grønvoll tied the ailing soldier to the sled and pulled him over a
rocky mountain. At times, Baalsrud's foot bled, and he passed out
from the pain. The journey took longer than Grønvoll expected, and
the men didn't have enough supplies to continue. They decided to
leave Baalsrud under the shelter of a large rock. They cut a hole in
the snowdrifts around it to better hide him.

Grønvoll then contacted resistance members he knew in the
nearby town of Manndalen. They knew the best route through
the mountains to Sweden. They would take Baalsrud from his new
hiding place and bring him to safety. But when the men searched for
his rocky shelter, they couldn't find it. After hearing this, Grønvoll
went back to look for the spot and found Baalsrud. He had somehow
survived alone in the snowy hideout for several days. Grønvoll gave
him food and said the men from Manndalen would come back
for him and arrange his trip to Sweden.

Another raging blizzard delayed the arrival of the Manndalen
rescuers. In his rock and snow cave shelter, Baalsrud watched the
snow pile up around him. He could barely sleep as pain and cold
tormented him. Finally, the resistance members from Manndalen
reached Baalsrud and put him on the sled. They headed for the
Swedish border. The recent snows and the mountainous terrain
made the trip slow, and Baalsrud's rescuers grew tired. One of the
men, Nigo, had friends in Sweden who owned reindeer. The animals
could pull the sled easier than the men could. Nigo set off to get
help. Meanwhile, the others built a wall of snow to protect Baalrsud
from the wind. Then they waited for Nigo to return with the reindeer.

People in Arctic regions have long used reindeer and sleds to travel across the snow-covered landscape.

Nigo returned with bad news—his friends couldn't come right away. But the other men sent a message to resistance members in the area. They managed to find reindeer that could pull Baalsrud. Finally, on June 1, Baalsrud reached the safety of Sweden.

At a hospital in Boden, a doctor examined Baalsrud. He now weighed just 80 pounds (36 kilograms). His feet still stank from the rotting flesh, but the doctor didn't have to amputate them. Baalsrud stayed in Sweden for several months to regain his strength. But even after all he had survived, he still wanted to defeat the Germans. He returned to Great Britain and helped train other commandos who were eager to free Norway from German occupation.

CRASH IN THE ARCTIC
THE SURVIVORS OF BOXTOP 22

In the distance, Captain John Couch could see the lights of the airfield where he would land his C-130 Hercules. On October 30, 1991, the aircraft, nicknamed Boxtop 22, was carrying five crewmembers, 13 passengers, and about 900 gallons (3,400 liters) of heating fuel to Canada's Ellesmere Island. The secret air base there, called Alert, was staffed by Canadian military forces. It's the most northerly settlement in the world, just a few hundred miles south of the North Pole.

The C-130 Hercules is one of the largest and most powerful planes in the world. The planes can carry up to 45,000 pounds (20,400 kg) of cargo.

The so-called polar night had darkened the late afternoon sky. That far north at that time of year, the sun offers a faint glow for just two hours around noon. The rest of the day, the sky is black. To save time, Captain Couch used a visual approach to Alert's runway instead of relying on the plane's instruments. With the clear, dark sky and the bright lights at the field, Couch thought the landing would be no problem. He received word from his navigator, Michael Moore, that he was clear to descend to 1,500 feet (457 m). But Moore had misread his radar screen. As Couch took Boxtop 22 lower, no one realized how close the plane was to the ground.

In the back of the plane, Sue Hillier had just mentioned how smooth she thought the flight was. Hillier, a hairdresser, was traveling to Alert to provide her services to the military staff there. Then, as the plane turned toward the left, it dropped suddenly. "We're going to crash!" someone yelled. An instant later, Hillier saw a rock pierce the bottom of the airplane. No one inside knew that one wing had clipped the top of a small mountain, sending the plane to the ground and hitting the rock Hillier saw rise toward her.

Boxtop 22 slid for almost 0.5 mile (0.8 km) over the snow and rocks. The bumpy glide on the ground broke the plane into three pieces. Most of the 18 people on board were thrown clear of the wreckage. The crash also ruptured the tanks holding the heating fuel. Hillier found herself still strapped in her seat in the snow. Her clothes were drenched with the fuel.

In the fragment of the plane that held the cockpit, a fire broke out. Couch and the rest of the flight crew managed to get out safely. But one passenger who had been sitting behind First Officer Joe Bales wasn't so lucky. Bales saw that logistics officer Judy Trepanier was on fire. He ran over to put out the flames, but it was too late to save her life.

THE DEAD AND THE INJURED

The survivors of the crash checked themselves and each other for injuries. Some had cuts and burns. Others had broken bones. A metal bar had smashed into Hillier's mouth, breaking a tooth and causing her to bite her tongue. When she tried to get out of her seat, Hillier felt a sharp stab of pain through her body. As Captain Wilma de Groot, a doctor, examined Hillier's injuries, the two women heard others crying out. Couch and the other surviving crew had learned that Corporal Roland Pitre had died from his injuries. Soon Master Warrant Officer Tom Jardine and Warrant Officer Robert Grimsley also died from their injuries.

The remaining survivors, except for Hillier and Bob Thomson, took cover under the broken wing of the plane. Hillier and Thomson couldn't move because of their serious injuries.

Thomson's back was broken, and Hillier had several broken bones. The other 11 huddled together to try to stay warm. Most of the survival gear the plane carried, including food, blankets, and warm sleeping bags, had burned in the fire or been lost in the snow. De Groot wondered how everyone would survive the extreme cold. Temperatures were dropping quickly, and the wind chill approached -75° F (-59° C). Every hour or so, de Groot called out the names of the survivors and waited for them to respond. She wanted to make sure they hadn't died in the cold darkness.

Meanwhile, Captain Couch used a tarp, sleeping bags, and snow to build a crude shelter for Hillier and Thomson. Couch explained to Hillier that the others were by the wing. But he assured her, "I won't leave you, Sue." Couch and Bales then built a small fire to provide some extra warmth for the two severely injured passengers. As Couch worked, Hillier could see that he was wearing only lightweight clothing. He had refused to take any of the warm clothing that had survived the crash so that others could wear it.

Couch and the rest of the crew stayed busy. Flight Engineer Paul West heard a plane overhead and tried to make radio contact with it. Meanwhile, Couch helped the others search for the survival gear. One valuable find were some special candies that were packed with calories. De Groot figured there were enough candies for everyone for just 12 hours.

West couldn't contact the other plane. However, an emergency locator device on Boxtop 22 had survived the crash. Its signal would put a rescue team into action. But the crash survivors had no way of knowing if the signal had been detected—or if a rescue team would arrive in time.

A COLD AND DEADLY NIGHT

After several hours passed, snow began falling around the crash site. The survivors who could walk or be carried were moved to the tail section of the plane. It seemed to offer more protection from the weather. But the falling snow soon turned into a howling blizzard. As the survivors shivered in the cold, some heard a plane fly overhead. But the thick cloud cover meant no one in the air could spot the crash site.

As he'd promised, Captain Couch continued checking on the two survivors separated from the others. First Officer Bales helped too. Hillier asked the captain if there was any news about when they might be rescued. All he could say was that help was surely on the way. Even as Hillier worried if she would live, or be paralyzed, she could see the cold was weakening Couch. At one point he told her, "We didn't see the hills," referring to the crash. As he spoke, his body shuddered violently. Hillier tried to reassure him that she knew it was an accident. "Nobody blames you," she said.

As the night wore on, West made brief radio contact with a rescue plane overhead. The rescue crew responded, saying that a ground team was on its way. The bad weather meant rescuers couldn't be sent by helicopter or parachute. Then, in the middle of the transmission, the batteries on the radio died. But at least everyone knew help was on the way.

The cold, though, got worse through night. In the tail section, the survivors stretched out on the plane's metal flooring. They kept moving so they wouldn't freeze to the floor. But their injuries made them cry out in pain. One survivor asked the others to kill him, thinking he wouldn't live until the rescuers came. The other survivors refused.

The rough arctic terrain of Canada's Ellesmere Island made it very difficult for rescuers to reach the crash survivors.

The extreme cold also claimed another victim. Without warm clothes, Captain Couch's frequent trips outside to check on Hillier and Thomson took its toll. On one of her roll calls, de Groot called out Couch's name. He didn't respond. She called out again, but there was nothing but silence. Bates crawled over to the captain and realized he was dead.

RESCUED AT LAST

Eleven people remained inside the freezing tail section as the storm continued to blow. Outside, Hillier and Thomson were still alive in their crude shelters as the snow piled up around them. By the morning of October 31, more than 30 hours after the crash, all the survivors were near death from hypothermia. But help was finally on the way. Above the crash site, a rescue team parachuted out of a Hercules plane and landed in the snow. They found some of the dead bodies in the snow before making their way to the tail section. "Anybody in there?" one of the rescuers called out, and they heard a mumbled response of "yes." Soon the rescuers were helping the wounded. Some of them cried as they realized they were saved.

De Groot told the rescuers there were two others out in the snow. Bales tried to direct the men to where Hillier and Thomson were. They were still alive the last time he'd checked. As the rescuers reached the spot he had indicated, they heard two voices: "Here! We are here!" Thomson moved his one good hand, poking at the tarp above him. That was enough for the rescuers to find them.

Within an hour, a team of ground rescuers reached the site in all-weather vehicles called Go-Tracks. They carried medical supplies to treat the wounded. Several hours later, the weather cleared enough for a helicopter to take the 13 survivors to Alert. All of them survived their wounds. In a sense, many of them had been lucky. The extreme cold had made conditions unbearable. However, it prevented the survivors' wounds and burns from becoming infected. They had nearly been frozen to death, but the cold had actually helped them survive.

DID YOU KNOW?

The men who found and saved the 13 survivors of the Boxtop 22 crash were members of the Canadian Forces Search and Rescue Technicians. These military personnel are also called SAR Techs. They operate across Canada and have often been called to rescue people in the Arctic. They are trained to reach remote areas by parachuting, swimming, or rock climbing to provide immediate medical care to those in need.

Canada's Search and Rescue Technicians are specially trained to carry out rescue missions in many difficult conditions and situations.

ADRIFT IN THE ICE
BOB BARTLETT AND THE *KARLUK* CREW

In 1913, while explorers crossed Antarctica, Vilhjalmur Stefansson had his eyes set on the opposite side of the world. He had already explored parts of the Canadian and Alaskan Arctic coasts. Now he wanted to go even farther north, in search of new lands near the North Pole. With money from the Canadian government, Stefansson organized a scientific expedition to explore the Beaufort Sea.

For the trip, Stefansson bought an old wooden fishing boat called the *Karluk*. The ship wasn't designed to sail in icy waters, but the price was cheap. For his captain, he chose Bob Bartlett, who had sailed earlier with Admiral Robert Peary to the Arctic. Peary recommended Bartlett to Stefansson. But when the captain first saw his new ship, he wasn't happy. Despite repairs that had been made, Bartlett doubted it would survive the voyage Stefansson had planned.

The *Karluk* left Victoria, British Columbia, on June 17, 1913. About two dozen people were on board, including scientists from several nations. Later, the ship picked up several Inuit people and a team of almost 30 sledge dogs. The ship sailed first for Nome, Alaska, before heading north for the Beaufort Sea.

For the *Karluk*'s crew and passengers, the voyage turned dangerous several weeks after leaving Nome. They crossed the Arctic Circle on July 27 and were met with stiff winds and rough seas. Snow began to fall a few days later. It was early in the year for such cold weather, even in the southern Arctic. Soon the crew spotted ice in the water. Captain Bartlett tried to find a path through it but had no luck. Finally, a shift in the wind's direction pushed the ice clear, and the *Karluk* sailed on.

Arctic explorer Captain Bob Bartlett in 1911

However, the ship soon came upon more ice and became stuck. The passengers and crew took time to get off the ship and explore the ice pack all around them. Some played soccer, while others tried out cross-country skis. On August 6, the ice shifted again, and the ship resumed its journey.

DRIFTING IN THE ICE

The *Karluk* continued to run into more ice, and the ship suffered damage as the ice packs crashed into it. Each time the ship encountered more ice and then worked itself free, Captain Bartlett criticized Stefansson for buying such a poor ship. But there was nothing the captain could do but try to keep the *Karluk* moving. By August 13, the ship was stuck in the ice for good. The only movement came when the ice pack surrounding the *Karluk* moved on its own. At times the ice-locked ship drifted 20 miles (32 km) in a single day.

The next month, Stefansson decided to take some men, dogs, and sledges off the ship to hunt for caribou. They left on September 20. But two days later a blizzard rolled in, with

Trapped in the ice, the Karluk *drifted westward for more than four months until it sank about 140 miles (225 km) northeast of Wrangel Island.*

winds reaching 60 miles (97 km) per hour. The storm pushed the *Karluk* farther to the west. From land, Stefansson and his party could no longer see the ship. The expedition leader decided to continue traveling south by dog sledge, to Point Barrow, Alaska.

Back on the *Karluk*, the ship drifted in the ice as the winds blew. After several days, Captain Bartlett ordered everyone to bring anything they had on the ice back on board the ship. Scientist William Laird McKinlay later wrote that "the gale was fiercer than ever, and drifting snow blotted out everything." The amount of sunlight each day was shrinking, and "the sense of insecurity, aggravated by the storm, was intensified by the eeriness of the dark."

Surrounded by ice, the *Karluk* drifted for months. The passengers and crew became bored, though Bartlett did let them go onto the ice at times. As time passed, the crew moved most of their supplies onto the ice. Bartlett worried that at some point the ice would crush the *Karluk*'s wooden hull and send the ship into the icy waters. The men built several shelters on the ice pack, using supplies from the ship and blocks of ice.

On January 10, 1914, Bartlett's decision to build the little village on the ice proved a wise one. The grating and crushing ice punched a hole in the ship's hull, and water poured in. The passengers and crew abandoned the ship. Early the next morning, they all watched the *Karluk* sink. Everyone then settled into their new home, which they nicknamed "Shipwreck Camp." Their shelters and several stoves helped protect them from the cold, with temperatures falling well below 0° F (-18° C). The men also relied on the help of an Inuit woman they called Auntie. She sewed furs and hides to make warm clothing for the crew.

THE PARTY SPLITS

Bartlett decided they should stay at the camp until the polar night ended and the sun returned. However, several of the men suggested first sending out a scouting party. Bartlett gave them permission to take some dogs and try to reach Wrangel Island. The island was close to Siberia, part of the Russian mainland in the Arctic. But before the men could leave, a blizzard hit the area, delaying the trip. As they waited out the storm, the men grew nervous at the loud noises of ice floes around them. The floes scraped and cracked open, leaving gaps into the freezing waters below.

Led by Bjarne Mamen, the scouting party finally left on January 21, with instructions to set up a camp on Wrangel Island. Several men would then return to bring the others to the camp. Meanwhile, the men at the new camp would hunt for meat and look for driftwood to build fires.

On February 3, Mamen and two Inuit men left the others in the scouting party and returned to the spot where the *Karluk* sank. But by then, three other men back at Shipwreck Camp had set off on their own. They were led by surgeon Alistair Mackay. They'd grown impatient and didn't want to wait for the scouting party to return from Wrangel Island.

But as it turned out, Mamen reported that the scouting party hadn't reached Wrangel Island after all. They'd made camp at Herald Island instead. It was about 38 miles (61 km) east of Wrangel and farther from the mainland. The men had gotten lost on their way to Wrangel, so they stopped at Herald, which was closer. Unfortunately, the small island offered none of the natural resources that Wrangel Island did.

Mamen had left four men on the edge of Herald Island before heading back. Bartlett decided to send another team to the island. When they returned, the team members reported that they couldn't reach Herald Island because the ice around it had melted. They also saw no sign of the first team that Mamen had left behind.

After the Karluk sank, the crew built Shipwreck Camp from the remains of the ship.

THE TRIP TO WRANGEL ISLAND

On February 19, Bartlett sent the first of two larger teams toward Wrangel Island. They were all going to leave Shipwreck Camp for good. Several weeks before, small teams of men and dogs had taken sledges filled with supplies and dropped them off along the route. One of those teams found Dr. Mackay and the other two men who had set off on their own. The three were in bad shape, struggling to survive in the cold and pulling their own supplies. They had left the camp without any dogs. Their odds of surviving were slim, but they refused any help. The men were never seen again.

Making the trek to Wrangel Island were the 17 surviving members of the original *Karluk* team. Over the following weeks, they avoided gaps in the ice, slept in igloos, and killed several polar bears. Along the way, the cracking ice continually threatened to send them and their supplies tumbling into the water. At times, they had to use ropes to pull their sledges up and over huge ridges of ice that blocked their path. Some ridges were more than 100 feet (30 m) high. When the group finally cleared the ridges, Ernest Chafe looked back and saw what he later called a "monster wall." But ahead, there was a "vast, almost level stretch of ice before us."

The team finally reached Wrangel Island on March 12. Several days later, Bartlett and an Inuit man named Kataktovick left to try to reach Siberia and find help to rescue the others. They took an indirect route, as Bartlett wanted to see if he could find any survivors from the first two teams that left Shipwreck Camp. He and Kataktovick traveled about 200 miles (322 km) but saw no signs of the others.

The two men slept in igloos and battled snow and wind as they made their way toward Siberia. They and the dogs pulling their

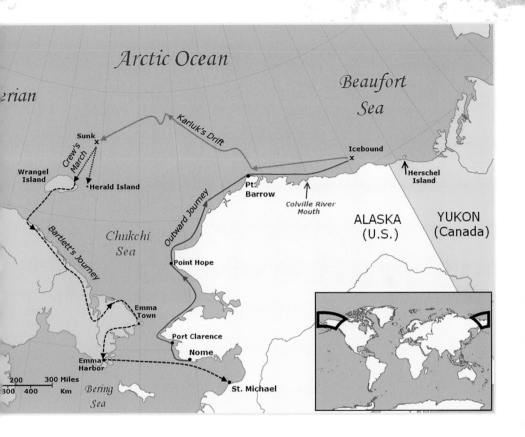

sledge had to get around or across a growing number of gaps in
the ice. Bartlett later called them "the most…treacherous of all
Arctic travelling."

REACHING SAFETY

On the night of April 4, Bartlett and Kataktovick stepped off
the ice sheet that linked Wrangel Island to the mainland. They
had reached Siberia. They camped for the night and found a small
village the next morning. The people there were called Chukchis,
and some invited the starving men into their home and fed them.
But Bartlett knew their trip wasn't over. They had to reach a larger
town where they could send a message back to Canada about the
survivors still on Wrangel Island.

Bob Bartlett (fifth from the left) and the surviving members of the Karluk *expedition onboard the* Bear *in September 1914*

With the help of other Chukchis and an American trader named Olsen, Bartlett and Kataktovick traveled for several weeks until they reached Emma Town. There, they met a Russian nobleman named Kleist who said he would take Bartlett to his home in Emma Harbor. From there, the captain could sail to Alaska. But Bartlett first needed to regain his strength and recover from an illness. In mid-May, he said goodbye to Kataktovick and traveled with Kleist. They reached Emma Harbor on May 16, and on May 21, Bartlett sailed for St. Michael, Alaska. From there, more than two months after leaving Wrangel Island, he was finally able to send a message to Canadian officials.

In the months after Bartlett left to get help, three men there had died. The food supply had run dangerously low, so the 14 remaining survivors ate local roots and at times pieces of walrus hide. Snow had started falling in September, and William McKinlay was convinced they would have to spend the winter there. But on September 7, he and several others spotted a ship off the coast. McKinlay realized that Bartlett's message had finally reached Canada.

In a state of shock, all McKinlay could think about was food. He and the others boarded the ship *King and Winge* and enjoyed a hot meal and bath. Soon, they transferred to another ship, the *Bear*. Bartlett was on board and was disappointed to hear that three men had died on Wrangel Island. But he and the other survivors were finally going home.

DID YOU KNOW?

More than 30 years before the *Karluk* sailed north, the USS *Jeannette* left San Francisco for the Arctic. Captain George Washington De Long and his crew of 33 men hoped to be the first to reach the North Pole. But as on the *Karluk*'s voyage, icy waters near Wrangel Island doomed the *Jeannette* and some of its crew. In September 1879, the ship became trapped in ice and drifted in the Arctic Ocean for almost two years. In June 1881, just before ice crushed their wooden ship, De Long and his men took all the supplies they could and escaped in three small boats. Hoping to reach Siberia, they pulled the boats over ice for almost three months until they reached open waters. At sea, one of the boats sank, killing all eight men on board. The other two boats reached land. But of the remaining 25 men, only 13 were eventually rescued. De Long and 11 other men all died of starvation and sickness before they were discovered.

A LONG ANTARCTIC WINTER
VICTOR CAMPBELL AND THE EASTERN PARTY

Robert Falcon Scott had a dream to become the first person to reach the South Pole. He set sail from Cardiff, Wales, on board the *Terra Nova* to achieve his goal in June 1910. But at a stop the following October in Melbourne, Australia, Scott learned that Norwegian explorer Roald Amundsen was pursuing the same goal. It would become a race to see who could reach the South Pole first.

On board the *Terra Nova* with Scott was Victor Campbell. He had served in the British navy and had spent time in Norway, where he learned how to cross-country ski. Campbell was in charge of a six-man scientific team called the Eastern Party. Their mission was to explore King Edward VII Land, which Scott had discovered and named during an earlier Antarctic expedition. Campbell's mission was to map the region and learn about the weather, ice, and wildlife there.

The *Terra Nova* reached Cape Evans, Antarctica, in January 1911. After unloading Scott's Western Party and their supplies, Campbell sailed on with the Eastern Party. Dr. George Levick, another member of the party, wrote that the team was going where no one had gone before, "and [we] do not know what we shall find. May it be land!"

Rather than dogs, the Eastern team would use ponies to pull their sledges. They also had a supply of frozen seals and penguins that could be used as food. Campbell's team sailed east in search of a place to land, but soon returned to Cape Evans to drop off their ponies. Campbell decided they weren't suitable for the coastal areas his team would explore.

Victor Campbell in 1910

Leaving Cape Evans once again, the Eastern party sailed
north to Cape Adare. Unlike King Edward VII Land, this area
had been explored before, but time was running out to set up
a winter camp. The cape had huts built by the earlier explorers
that would provide shelter as the Eastern party waited out the
winter. Campbell and his team unloaded their supplies, and the
Terra Nova sailed on. It wouldn't return for almost a year.

THE MISSING SHIP

During that time, the Eastern party worked to strengthen the huts they'd found. They killed birds called skuas for additional meat. And they sat through ferocious blizzards that struck Cape Adare. When the polar summer came that October, the men began to explore the area. In January 1912, the *Terra Nova* returned and took the team to Evans Coves, south of Cape Adare. The six men once again unloaded their gear and set out to explore the area's glaciers and mountains. They traveled with their two sledges and slept in tents. Their time at Evans Coves would be short, as the *Terra Nova* was scheduled to pick them up on February 18.

When that day came, the men scanned the Ross Sea for signs of the ship. Several days passed, but the *Terra Nova* didn't arrive.

Terra Nova *in Antarctica in 1911*

However, strong winds did, which got stronger by the day. The team began to think that the ship might not reach them before winter. They realized they would have to stretch out their food supplies. After several weeks passed without the ship's arrival, the men were getting weak from lack of food. They began hunting seals and penguins to build up a supply of meat.

Strong winds kept the men in their tents some days, and one powerful blast ripped Campbell's tent. Using axes and a shovel, they carved out a shelter in a huge bank of snow. By March 7, the men realized the *Terra Nova* wouldn't make it to Evans Cove. They would have to spend the winter there with their supplies running low. They moved some of their food and equipment into their new snow cave, with strong winds knocking them over as they walked. In his diary, Raymond Priestly wrote, "We are feeling terribly fed up with things."

The seals and penguins grew harder to find as winter approached. So it seemed lucky when Frank Browning killed a seal. Even luckier was finding several dozen fish in its throat and stomach that were mostly whole, which the men eagerly ate.

As April came, the men's limited diet began to affect their health. They experienced digestive problems. Most also suffered frostbite from exposure to the extreme cold whenever they left their snow cave. Some of their clothing also began to fall apart, offering them even less protection from the cold.

DID YOU KNOW?

The men killed seals for an additional food source. Seals have a thick layer of fat called blubber that keeps them and other sea mammals warm in freezing waters. The blubber also stores protein and other nutrients. At Cape Adare, the Eastern party ate some blubber raw and also mixed it with seal meat. The men melted some of the fat to make a fuel to use for cooking and light. But the heavy, greasy smoke created by the burning fat sometimes choked them. It also turned their skin and the walls of their snow cave black.

A LONG, COLD WINTER

In May, heavy snows fell and drifted against the cave. The drifts blocked the chimney that vented the smoke from the team's fires. As the men developed headaches, they realized they were running out of fresh air. Campbell used a shovel to clear a new pathway for the smoke to escape.

As the winter dragged on, the men had little to do other than cook their meals and carry in more supplies when the wind let up. At times, they sang songs to pass the time, or talked about the food they would eat when they finally left their isolated winter home. They held onto the hope that the *Terra Nova* would still return.

While spending the winter in a snow cave, the men's skin and clothing became coated with greasy smoke from burning blubber.

In July the men found and killed several more seals to add to their food supply. They welcomed the additional meat, but the long weeks of being stuck inside the snow cave left them frustrated. Dr. Levick said that at times, he felt "inclined to smash the walls of the cave open & get out."

Time dragged on as the men tried to remain hopeful that they would survive the winter. As September began, they all became sick while strong winds howled outside. At times, they broke off pieces of ice from their cave to provide fresh water. They also knew they had to prepare to leave the cave and head to the base at Cape Evans. They couldn't count on the *Terra Nova* to return for them.

THE HARD TREK TO SAFETY

By the end of September 1912, the Antarctic spring was approaching, but heavy snow still pounded Cape Adare. Regardless, the men knew they had to try to find a way home. On September 30, Campbell and the others set off with two sledges loaded with food and gear. Through the winter months, they had saved some special food to prepare for this trip. Now the men enjoyed meals that sometimes included chocolate and hard biscuits.

In spite of the hardships they suffered, Campbell's Eastern Party survived and returned to Cape Evans in November 1912.

The snow continued as the men made slow progress across the ice and snow. Some members of the team were still sick, and frostbite was another problem. As October went on, the men weren't sure they had enough food to last the whole journey. The hard work of pulling the sledges required great energy, and the shortage of food sometimes left them drained. They killed some penguins and an occasional seal along the way. But by the end of October, they were running out of food. Their spirits lifted when they found a store of supplies left by earlier explorers. It included biscuits, sugar, butter, and other food. They also found a list that mentioned other storage depots scattered along the route to Cape Evans.

Even with the promise of more food ahead, the men still faced difficulties. One of their sledges fell apart along the way. The other broke down a few days later. In early November, the team had to march across sea ice on foot, but at least they knew they were close to Cape Evans.

On November 6, the men reached a hut on the cape where two members of the larger team were living. Campbell and the others were finally safe. They had plenty of supplies, and the men could sleep in real beds. Two months later, in January 1913, they spotted the *Terra Nova* sailing toward them. They would soon be on their way home to tell their incredible tale of surviving through an extreme winter in Antarctica.

TRAPPED IN THE ICE
ERNEST SHACKLETON'S DOOMED EXPEDITION

With a crew of 27, Ernest Shackleton boarded the wooden sailing ship *Endurance* to make his third voyage to Antarctica. He had traveled there in 1901 with Robert Falcon Scott, trying but failing to reach the South Pole. Then in 1908, Shackleton returned as the leader of another expedition that tried to reach the pole. That mission was also unsuccessful.

Now in August 1914, Roald Amundsen and Scott had already reached the South Pole. Shackleton instead had a new mission—to lead the British Imperial Trans-Antarctic Expedition. The goal was to cross the entire icy continent, all 1,800 miles (2,900 km) of it, with a stop at the pole. It was an ambitious plan—something that nobody had accomplished before.

From England, the *Endurance* sailed first to Argentina and then headed to South Georgia Island. This island was used as a base for whaling operations in the southern Atlantic Ocean. From there, the ship headed for Antarctica's Weddell Sea. Shackleton planned to come ashore at Vahsel Bay. A second ship would then sail on to McMurdo Sound on the other side of the continent. The crew from that ship would leave food depots for Shackleton's team to use in their final march across Antarctica.

The *Endurance* sailed from South Georgia Island on December 5, 1914. But before long, the ship encountered a huge spread of ice on the water's surface. Shackleton was surprised to find so much thick ice so far from Antarctica. By January 1915, his ship was trapped in the ice.

As the ice drifted and carried the *Endurance* along, the men could sometimes see land not far away. But they had no chance of reaching it as long as they were locked in the pack ice. By February, Shackleton began to think that he and his crew would be stuck in the ice through the Antarctic winter. Wind and the shifting ice carried them along, but they never got close enough to the shore to leave the ship.

Though it was summertime in Antarctica, the Endurance *became trapped in the ice in January 1915.*

THE END OF ENDURANCE

As winter set in, the crew moved their sledge dogs onto the ice that surrounded them. The men sometimes left the ship to hunt seals. On board, they heard large floes of ice grinding together. At times the collisions hurled large chunks of ice out of the water.

The *Endurance* was caught in its icy trap for almost 10 months. At times, it tilted dramatically, sending supplies, dogs, and men sliding across its decks. In late October, Shackleton realized that the ice would soon crush the ship. The beams had been cracking for weeks, and water was starting to fill the ship. Shackleton later wrote that the beams snapped "with a noise like heavy gun-fire." On October 27, he ordered the men and dogs to abandon ship. The crew took with them all the supplies they could carry and three lifeboats.

About a mile away from the ship, Shackleton and his men set up camp on an ice floe. They stayed there for two months, and Shackleton called the spot Ocean Camp. From there, on November 21, the men watched the *Endurance* sink below the ice. Shackleton saw the bow, or front, of the ship plunge down first. He later wrote, "she gave one quick dive and the ice closed over her forever." Although the ship had been useless for weeks, Shackleton thought the loss of their ship left the men lonelier and more hopeless than before.

While at Ocean Camp, the men hunted each day for penguins and seals. At night they slept in tents. Winds continued to push the ice floe along. Shackleton hoped they would eventually get close enough to land to reach the shore on the lifeboats.

The Endurance *drifted for several months before it was finally crushed and sank below the ice in November 1915.*

SEARCHING FOR A NEW "HOME"

However, in December 1915 there was no land in sight, and the floe was starting to melt. The men decided to walk over the ice in search of open waters. They dragged two of the lifeboats with them. Crossing soft patches of ice, Shackleton wrote, the progress was "slow and tiring." After just a few days, Shackleton gave up on his plan, and the men settled on a new ice floe. They called the spot Patience Camp. Since they hadn't gone far, Shackleton sent some of the men back to Ocean Camp to retrieve the lifeboat and supplies they had left behind.

As time passed, the men grew bored. They felt like prisoners on the ice. Their main activities were hunting and then eating their kill. When blizzards blew in, the men were forced to stay in their tents. By March 1916, the ice floe had shrunk in size. While the men could see land, they never drifted close enough to it.

By April the wind and currents combined to create openings in the ice. The men finally had to get in their boats and search for land, even if it was only an island. On April 9 the crew began to sail through the freezing waters. Spray from rough seas soon covered the men in a thin layer of ice. The small boats also encountered thicker sea ice that slowed their journey.

The conditions grew worse, and the cold winds kept the men awake at night. Many suffered from frostbite. One morning, the men had to eat frozen dog food for breakfast. On April 14, the boats sailed toward Elephant Island, about 40 miles (64 km) away. For a time, strong winds separated the three boats. They found each other again, but a powerful storm and subzero temperatures made for an awful night. As water flooded the boats, the men struggled to bail it out so the vessels wouldn't sink. The next day, the boats finally reached the safety of Elephant Island.

Using lumber salvaged from the Endurance, the men built Ocean Camp on an ice floe nearby.

While Shackleton and his men had finally reached solid ground, their troubles were far from over. Some of the men were too weak to leave the boats on their own and had to be carried. The party finally reached a spot that Shackleton named Cape Wild. The men tried to set up shelters, but high winds knocked down one tent and blew away some supplies. Plus, falling and drifting snow kept covering the men and their gear. In spite of their struggles, Shackleton later wrote that he believed "the camp was safe" and the men would benefit from the "opportunity for rest and recuperation."

SEARCHING FOR HELP

Soon, though, conditions became desperate. The team knew that the chances of a ship finding them on Elephant Island were slim. Shackleton decided that he and the healthiest men should take one of the boats and seek help. On April 24 they set off for South Georgia Island.

However, their destination was about 800 miles (1,287 km) away. The small boat, just a little over 22 feet (6.7 m) long, was not equipped for such a long voyage across cold waters. The men's clothing and sleeping bags were quickly soaked, and Shackleton later wrote that the men "fought the seas and the winds and at the same time had a daily struggle to keep ourselves alive."

As they sailed, a thick layer of ice weighed the down boat, slowing its progress. The men took turns chipping at the ice. One day, a huge tidal wave appeared out of nowhere. It swamped the boat and almost sank it. But the men clung tightly to the boat. They bailed out the water and sailed on.

Frank Worsley, who had captained the *Endurance*, tried to steer the boat through the high winds and rough seas. At night, when the sky was clear, he used his knowledge of the stars to guide him. Despite the difficulties the men faced, Worsley was able to get the boat to South Georgia Island after 16 days at sea.

Shackleton and five other men set sail from Elephant Island and braved rough seas to find help for the rest of the crew.

THE LAST PUSH TO SAFETY

Even after reaching an island where they could find help, the men's struggle still wasn't over. They'd have to sail another 150 miles (241 km) to find a settlement. Shackleton instead decided to take a shortcut across the island with two of the healthiest men. But it was no easy walk. The three had to cross ice fields and mountains. Exhausted from all they had already experienced, they made slow progress. Twice they had to turn back and take another path after reaching steep cliffs with no way down.

On another mountain, about 4,500 feet (1,372 m) high, the three men once again faced a cliff. With temperatures plunging, Shackleton decided they had to risk climbing down. For a time, they slid on a crude toboggan they made out of rope. Finally, after another grueling 36-hour hike, the three men reached a whaling station. Their appearance shocked the first people they found. The survivors' clothes were ripped and their skin was blackened from the smoke of blubber fires. They hadn't bathed in months, so they smelled bad as well.

But the men had survived almost 18 months since the *Endurance* had become trapped in the ice. Shackleton soon sent a ship to rescue the rest of the party. It reached Elephant Island on August 30, 1916. Somehow, all 22 men there had survived for four and a half months after Shackleton left. The experience of the Shackleton expedition remains one of the most amazing stories of people surviving in the world's harshest polar regions.

The rest of Shackleton's crew waited at Camp Wild on Elephant Island. They were finally rescued more than four months after their leader left to get help.

DID YOU KNOW?

In 2019 a team of scientists studying Antarctica hoped to find the wreckage of the *Endurance*. The scientists had a small remote-controlled submarine they hoped to use to locate the ship. But the sub was lost under an ice floe that February. The scientists tried to locate the sub and rescue it, but as the weather grew worse, they had to give up. A spokesman for the scientific mission said the experience with the sub was "a reminder of what Shackleton and his team experienced in terms of the harshness of the environment."

GLOSSARY

avalanche—a large amount of snow, ice, or rock that moves quickly down a mountain

blubber—a thick layer of fat that helps sea mammals stay warm in cold water

commando—a soldier specially trained to carry out missions in enemy territory

crevasse—a large gap in a glacier that is sometimes hidden by a layer of snow

depot—a collection of supplies left along a route that explorers plan to take

expedition—a journey or voyage made for a specific purpose, such as scientific research or exploration

floe—a floating sheet of ice

gangrene—a serious infection that occurs when body tissues die and begin to decay

glacier—a large, slowly moving sheet of ice

hypothermia—a life-threatening condition that occurs when a person's body temperature falls several degrees below normal

Inuit—people native to Alaska and some other Arctic regions

sastrugi—ridges formed on hard snow by wind

sledge—a strong, heavy sled

wind chill—the combined effect of temperature and wind on exposed skin

READ MORE

Bailey, Diane. *Polar Exploration: Courage and Controversy.* Broomall, PA: Mason Crest, 2018.

Mara, Wil. *Antarctica.* New York: Children's Press, 2017.

Olson, Tod. *Lost in the Antarctic: The Doomed Voyage of the Endurance.* New York: Scholastic Press, 2019.

INTERNET SITES

14 of History's Greatest Polar Explorers
https://www.mnn.com/earth-matters/animals/photos/13-of-historys-greatest-polar-explorers/into-the-icy-unknown#top-desktop

Exploration: Arctic
https://nsidc.org/cryosphere/seaice/exploration/arctic.html

The Great Escape of Jan Baalsrud
https://www.smh.com.au/lifestyle/the-great-escape-of-jan-baalsrud-20160330-gnts49.html

The Most Terrible Polar Expedition Ever
https://www.smithsonianmag.com/history/the-most-terrible-polar-exploration-ever-douglas-mawsons-antarctic-journey-82192685/

Shackleton's Voyage of Endurance
https://www.pbs.org/wgbh/nova/shackleton/

SOURCE NOTES

p. 9, "a fight with Death." David Roberts, *Alone on the Ice: The Greatest Survival Story in the History of Exploration*. New York: W. W. Norton, 2013, p. 211.

p. 21, "We're here to take care of you, Jan." Astrid Karlsen Scott and Tore Haug. *Defiant Courage: A WWII Epic of Escape and Endurance*. New York: Skyhorse, 2010, p. 196.

p. 25, "We're going to crash!" Ron Arias, "Hell Frozen Over," *People*, November 25, 1991, https://people.com/archive/hell-frozen-over-vol-36-no-20/, accessed May 16, 2019.

p. 27, "I won't leave you, Sue." Robert Mason Lee. *Death and Deliverance: The True Story of an Airplane Crash at the North Pole*. Golden, CO: Fulcrum Publishing, 1993, p. 89.

p. 28, "We didn't see the hills." *Ibid.*, p. 151.

p. 28, "Nobody blames you." *Ibid.*, p. 153.

p. 30, "Anybody in there?...Yes" *Ibid.*, p. 243.

p. 30, "Here! We are here!" *Ibid.*, p. 250.

p. 35, "the gale was fiercer than ever..." William Laird McKinlay, *The Last Voyage of the Karluk: A Survivor's Memoir of Arctic Disaster*. New York: St. Martin's Griffin, 1999, p. 35.

p. 38, "monster wall...vast, almost level stretch..." Jennifer Niven. *The Ice Master: The Doomed 1913 Voyage of the Karluk*. New York: Hyperion, 2000, p. 186.

p. 39, "the most . . . treacherous..." Jenny Higgins, "The Karluk Disaster," Heritage Newfoundland and Labrador, https://www.heritage.nf.ca/articles/exploration/karluk-disaster.php, accessed May 17, 2019.

p. 42, "and [we] do not know..." Meredith Hooper, *The Longest Winter: Scott's Other Heroes*. Berkeley, CA: Counterpoint, 2010, p. 74.

p. 45, "We are feeling terribly fed up with things." *Ibid.*, p. 216.

p. 47, "inclined to smash the walls..." *Ibid.*, p. 251.

p. 52, "with a noise like heavy gun-fire" Michael Smith, *Shackleton: By Endurance We Conquer*. London: Oneworld, 2014, p. 298.

p. 52, "she gave one quick dive..." Ernest Shackleton, *South: The Story of Shackleton's Last Expedition, 1914-1917*. New York: The Macmillan Company, 1920, p. 99.

p. 54, "slow and tiring." *Ibid.*, p. 106.

p. 55, "the camp was safe...opportunity for rest..." *Ibid.*, p. 157.

p. 59, "a reminder of what Shackleton..." Emily Dixon, "Antarctic Expedition to Find Shackleton's Lost *Endurance* Loses Its Own Submarine to the Ice," CNN, February 15, 2019, https://www.cnn.com/travel/article/antarctic-shackleton-expedition-called-off-scli-intl/index.html, accessed June 10, 2019.

SELECT BIBLIOGRAPHY

Arias, Ron. "Hell Frozen Over." *People*, November 25, 1991, https://people.com/archive/hell-frozen-over-vol-36-no-20/, accessed May 16, 2019.

Dash, Mike. "The Most Terrible Polar Expedition Ever." Smithsonian.com, January 27, 2012, https://www.smithsonianmag.com/history/the-most-terrible-polar-exploration-ever-douglas-mawsons-antarctic-journey-82192685/, accessed February 28, 2019.

Dixon, Emily. "Antarctic Expedition to Find Shackleton's Lost Endurance Loses Its Own Submarine to the Ice." CNN, February 15, 2019, https://www.cnn.com/travel/article/antarctic-shackleton-expedition-called-off-scli-intl/index.html, accessed June 10, 2019.

Higgins, Jenny. "The Karluk Disaster." Heritage Newfoundland and Labrador, https://www.heritage.nf.ca/articles/exploration/karluk-disaster.php, accessed May 17, 2019.

Hooper, Meredith. *The Longest Winter: Scott's Other Heroes*. Berkeley, CA: Counterpoint, 2011.

Jones, Deborah. "The School of Hard Knocks." *Globe and Mail*, September 18, 2006, https://www.theglobeandmail.com/news/national/the-school-of-hard-knocks/article968720/, accessed May 17, 2019.

Kolker, Robert. "The Great Escape of Jan Baalsrud." *The Sydney Morning Herald*, April 1, 2016, https://www.smh.com.au/lifestyle/the-great-escape-of-jan-baalsrud-20160330-gnts49.html, accessed March 15, 2019.

Lee, Robert Mason. *Death and Deliverance: The True Story of an Airplane Crash at the North Pole*. Golden, CO: Fulcrum Publishing, 1993.

Log Books of the United States Navy, 19th and 20th Centuries: USS *Jeannette*, https://www.naval-history.net/OW-US/Jeannette/USS_Jeannette-1879-1880.htm, accessed May 14, 2019.

McKinlay, William Laird. *The Last Voyage of the* Karluk: *A Survivor's Memoir of Arctic Disaster*. New York: St. Martin's Griffin, 1999.

Niven, Jennifer. *The Ice Master: The Doomed 1913 Voyage of the* Karluk. New York: Hyperion, 2000.

Roberts, David. *Alone on the Ice: The Greatest Survival Story in the History of Exploration*. New York: W. W. Norton, 2013.

Scott, Astrid Karlsen, and Tore Haug. *Defiant Courage: A WWII Epic of Escape and Endurance*. New York: Skyhorse, 2010.

Shackleton, Ernest. *South: The Story of Shackleton's Last Expedition, 1914-1917*. New York: The Macmillan Company, 1920.

Shackleton's Voyage of Endurance. PBS, *Nova*, https://www.pbs.org/wgbh/nova/shackleton/, accessed June 8, 2019.

Smith, Michael. *Shackleton: By Endurance We Conquer*. London: Oneworld, 2014.

INDEX

ABOUT THE AUTHOR

Michael Burgan has written numerous books for children and young adults during his nearly 20 years as a freelance author. Many of his books have focused on U.S. history, geography, and world leaders. He has also written fiction and adapted classic novels for children. Michael graduated from the University of Connecticut with a degree in history. He lives in Santa Fe, New Mexico.